HAYNES EXPLAINS
THE MIDLIFE CRISIS

Owners' Workshop Manual

© Haynes Publishing • Written by **Boris Starling**

Published in September 2019

A catalogue record for this book is available from the British Library

ISBN 978 1 78521 664 0

Haynes Publishing, Sparkford, Yeovil,
Somerset BA22 7JJ, UK
Tel: +44 (0) 1963 440635
Website: www.haynes.com

Haynes North America, Inc.,
861 Lawrence Drive, Newbury Park,
California 91320, USA

Printed and bound in Malaysia

Cover image from Getty Images

Illustrations taken from the
Haynes Rover 820, 825 & 827
Owners Workshop Manual

Written by **B**
Edit
Desi

D0475871

Safety first!

The midlife crisis is almost by definition not a place of safety. For a man, the four traditional 'M's of the crisis – motorbike, Maserati, marathon and mistress – are all likely to be injurious to his health in one way or another. And if you think falling off while doing the cones bit in your motorbike test is humiliating, you've clearly never stalled a Maserati at a busy intersection, run 26 miles dressed as a giant strawberry, or had your wife group message all your friends with a comprehensive list of your manifold shortcomings in and out of the sack.

Working facilities

Both men and women are susceptible to a midlife crisis, though men tend to get it earlier (43 vs. 44) and have it last longer (3–10 years vs. 2–5 years). When the crisis is over, women will often look back with pride at the way they handled it, whereas men will cover their eyes with their hand, shake their heads slowly and make a low keening noise like a distressed Wookiee. 'Was it really that bad?' they may ask. No, mate, it wasn't. It was worse.

Contents

Introduction

The midlife crisis is not a new phenomenon. Dante kicked off *The Divine Comedy* in 1308 with the words 'midway upon the journey of our life, I found myself within a forest dark, for the straightforward pathway had been lost.' In the first part of *The Divine Comedy* he journeys to Hell, or, as many midlifers have called it, Brent Cross shopping centre on a Bank Holiday Monday.

The actual phrase 'midlife crisis', however, wasn't coined until 1965, when the psychologist Elliott Jaques published 'Death and the Mid-life Crisis'. Like Dante and his Inferno,

Elliott was clearly a fan of picking the most morbid title possible. How about 'Fluffy Unicorns and the Mid-life Crisis', Elliott, you miserable bastard?

It's no coincidence that this came out at a time of great social change, including but not limited to the rise of feminism, civil rights, counterculture and self-expression. And the real USP of a midlife crisis was (and remains) its one-size-fits-all nature. You can have one if you've achieved too much but of the wrong sort, if you haven't achieved enough, if you're happily married, if you're unhappily unmarried and so on. All you need to have a midlife crisis is to be middle-aged.

That said, the midlife crisis is getting later and later, purely because people are living longer and longer. In times past, when you might be lucky to reach 50 (this was the average life expectancy in the UK as recently as 1900), a midlife crisis could start not long after puberty. What is now midlife was once the endgame, before the rise of diets, fitness programmes, kale smoothies and the like, which might not make you live to 120 but will certainly make you feel like it. Those who are now in their forties and fifties can reasonably expect to live to beyond 80: one in three of their children will probably hit 100 (if global warming hasn't done for the planet first, that is).

About this manual

Haynes Explains The Midlife Crisis examines the causes, symptoms and possible treatments for the crisis. This book has also tried to strike a balance between being amusing – it'll be a long time before the battle between open-top car and hair weave is anything less than hilarious – and practical, because midlife crises are real, they can cause great pain not just for the sufferers but for their families and friends too, and they are no respecter of colour, wealth or creed.

⚠ Dimensions, weights and capacities

Overall height
Of the new hair weave which looks like Monsanto have been
planting crops on your shiny bald pate:.. 13.14mm
Of the Porsche Boxster which will seriously test just how strong
the roots of that weave are when you drive it with the roof down: 1,281mm
Of the basketball hoop at which you attempt a slam dunk before
spending the next month recovering from a torn hamstring: 3,050mm

Overall weight
Of an average man aged 23:... 75kg
Of an average man aged 43:... 80kg
Of an average man aged 45 once the midlife crisis has kicked in: 70kg
Of an average man aged 65 once he's long over all that midlife
malarkey and simply no longer gives too much of a toss:............................ 80kg again

Consumption
Aged 23: ....   full English breakfast: Big Mac meal with extra fries for lunch;
....   chicken tikka masala and pilau rice for dinner; 10 pints to drink.
Aged 45: ....   porridge and fruit for breakfast; salmon, pasta and quinoa for lunch;
....   chicken and vegetables for dinner; water and electrolytes to drink.

Engine
Stroke: ....   what you're liable to have if you don't start getting fit, like right now.
....   Heightened stress and lower metabolisms do not good bedfellows
....   make, Mr You're-Not-21-Any-More-You-Really Aren't.
Power: ....   295bhp (Porsche Boxster); 459bhp (Corvette Stingray);
....   661bhp (Ferrari 488).
Bore: ....   you, mainly, for going on and on about how life hasn't turned out the
....   way you expected, and in turn expecting everyone else to listen for
....   hours on end when all they want to do is get in their own sports
....   cars and drive home to their much younger girlfriends because,
....   you know, communal crisis and all that.

Worn parts

It's not hard to know when you've reached midlife. Your body tells you. And it doesn't just tell you once, quietly and politely. It tells you time and again, as loudly and rudely as possible. Hey! You! You're getting older – but, crucially, not yet so old that you can't remember what it was like to be young. It's the midlife equivalent of the myth of Tantalus, who was made to stand in a pool of water beneath a fruit tree. The fruit was just out of reach, and the water would recede whenever he tried to drink it. That's your youth, still visible but never again to be experienced.

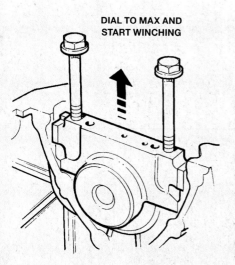

DIAL TO MAX AND START WINCHING

FIG 15•1 **DIY FACELIFT FOR THE MIDLIFE CRISIS SUFFERER**

Almost every part of you begins to wear out in middle age:

Your brain
You find yourself having mild 'senior moments', when you walk into a room and forget what you came in for.

Your eyes
You begin to need reading glasses, but sometimes you can't remember where you put them (see previous point.) Clue: try the top of your head first.

Your hair
This is covered more fully later on – no hairdresser has ever gone out of business by overestimating a middle-aged man's attitude to his hair – but suffice to say that, of all the ways in which time is a cruel mistress, the way it can transform a lad's bonce from Lionel Richie to Right Said Fred over a decade or two is right up there.

Your chin
Whereas many body parts are in one way or another diminishing, your chin may choose to buck the trend by becoming larger, perhaps deciding it enjoys its existence so much that it would like a twin with which to share things, or even reckon that being one of triplets is all the rage now.

Your ears

I said 'your ears'. NO! YOUR EARS!

Your waist

Well, technically it could be that you've inadvertently put all your trousers onto boilwash and they've shrunk, but that's like copying someone else's exam paper: you're only cheating yourself. Left unchecked, you can have more spare tyres than Pirelli down there. And the effort of standing up straight with all that to lug really knackers...

... your back

As does sitting down for long periods, which you can do in middle age as you've weathered two decades of Borgia-like office politics to become a company director, which means that you can make everyone else run around like you used to. And you have a corner office with a good view, which means you can look out of the window to break up the endless games of computer Solitaire you play.

Your bladder

In your 20s, being up several times in the night is something to smirk about. In your 40s, it's the well-trodden path from bedroom to bathroom: a situation exacerbated by the fact that, in the words of Alan Partridge (poster boy for every male midlife crisis), 'I never thought, when I was in my 20s, that I'd have to push.'

Everything else

Whenever you move up or down – something which you used to take so for granted that you could do it in silence – now you make a noise. A grunt, a sigh, a wince, an exhale. It becomes an automatic response, sound with movement, like those tennis players who every time they hit a ball go 'ah-AH!' really loudly and then smash their racket when the umpire gives them a code violation. You settle down on the sofa at 9 p.m. to watch a programme and wake two hours later to a *Newsnight* presenter staring accusingly at you.

IT LOOKED BAD IN MEDIEVAL TIMES...

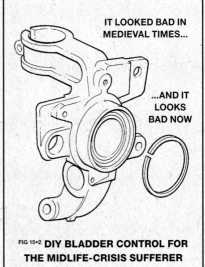

...AND IT LOOKS BAD NOW

FIG 15•2 **DIY BLADDER CONTROL FOR THE MIDLIFE-CRISIS SUFFERER**

CPU malfunctions

It's not just physical changes which herald a midlife crisis, but mental ones too. The genesis of any midlife question is always a question – not the kind of questions asked by your children ('why is a table not a fish?'), or your mate in the pub ('do you think 3-5-2 is really Southgate's best formation?'), or your spouse on your return from said pub ('what kind of time do you call this?'), but by philosophers since ancient times. 'Why?', basically. 'Why am I doing this?' Is this all there is to life?' And these questions can't be answered simply by some faux-inspirational internet meme of a glorious sunset and uplifting words.

Sufferers tend to feel the following:

a) That they don't know who they are anymore, and not in a temporary drunken amnesia kind of way either. Their role in life may be changing, with children growing older and more independent at one end and parents growing older but less independent at the other.

b) That they're stuck in a rut, doing the same old thing not just day in day out but week in week out, month in month out and year in year out. This belief is particularly prevalent among those packed into the 0728 from Broxbourne every morning.

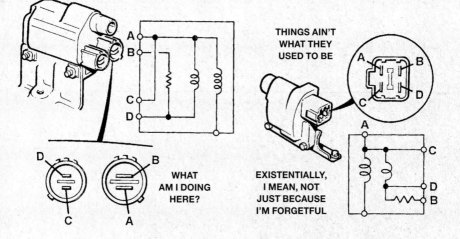

THINGS AIN'T WHAT THEY USED TO BE

WHAT AM I DOING HERE?

EXISTENTIALLY, I MEAN, NOT JUST BECAUSE I'M FORGETFUL

FIG 15•3 **REWIRING AFTER 40: CHANGING THOUGHT PATTERNS IN MIDLIFE**

c) That they begin to regret the path they didn't take, not least on the grounds of the old adage that it's better to regret something you have done rather than something you haven't. (Those who've ever taken the 'eat this hotter-than-the-sun phaal and get the rest of your meal free' challenge at the local curry house may disagree with this.) This untaken path might be a more rewarding job, a different place to have lived or a different person to have married.

d) That time is running out, or that more time has passed than they thought. A popular thought experiment invites you to take away your age from the year of your birth and see what was happening in the world at that time. If, for example, you were born in 1968 and it's now 2019, that would take you back to 1917 and still with a year of World War I to run. If that doesn't depress you, nothing will. Why on earth this thought experiment is popular is a mystery. It should be banned.

e) That they suffer mood swings, often extreme and without warning: one minute fine, the next snappy without any apparent reason (or at least no proportionate reason). To which, of course, any octogenarian would say 'at least you're only cantankerous half the time.'

WARNING

Not getting enough sleep. This is partly a physical thing too, of course – all those nocturnal trips to the bathroom – but also a sign of preoccupation and worry. No problem seems better at two in the morning than it did at two in the afternoon.

f) That they feel apathetic, down in the dumps or actively depressed. The latter is a different kettle of fish from the first two and requires professional help (and, in fairness, clinical depression is certainly not the sole preserve of the middle-aged). The one thing guaranteed not to work here is someone saying 'cheer up'. Just as no drunk person in the history of the world has ever agreed with the simple proposition 'I think you've had enough, mate,' so too has no one ever cheered up because someone has told them to.

g) That they're thinking about death or dying more than before. Sometimes they read obituaries more avidly than any other part of the paper (which in itself might not help: there's nothing like reading about a wartime hero who carried his own severed legs across Poland in 1944 to make you feel not so much beta male as omega male).

In the workshop

We spend more waking hours at work than we do at any single other activity (unless your area of employment is, ahem, adult films, in which case your job is also your hobby). How we feel about our jobs therefore has a huge effect on our mental state. When we're younger, and maybe grateful to have a job at all, work can be simply a way of earning money to pay for all the fun stuff. When we're older and retired, work has come and gone.

On the face of it, middle age can seem the best of both worlds: senior and well-paid enough to have made the slog worthwhile, yet still young enough to find it rewarding. But often the opposite is true. The only thing harder than making it to the top of the corporate ladder is staying there: management brings its own pressures, when it's not just your own livelihood you're responsible for but other people's too, and the constant need to ride the whitewater rapids of office politics could sap the energy from the hardiest soul.

Men and women in midlife worry about younger people taking their jobs. That bright young thing you're mentoring today will be sizing up your chair tomorrow. Those late-night stints they pull to help finish a project while you're at a school play will quickly turn from helpful team player to ambitious shark. And all the time you're looking over your shoulder at them, you have half an eye on your friends who make more money than you and go on better holidays than you do. Retirement plans? You'll be lucky! At this rate they'll be carrying you out of the office feet first.

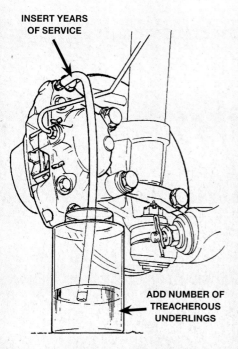

INSERT YEARS OF SERVICE

ADD NUMBER OF TREACHEROUS UNDERLINGS

FIG 15•4 **OFFICE POLITICS NAVIGATION DEVICE**

⚠ Parable of the Mexican fisherman

You read the contemporary parable of the Mexican fisherman, and you think he's got a point. The parable goes something like this:

An American businessman is on a remote Mexican beach when a fisherman returns to shore with his catch: a handful of yellowfin tuna.

'Can I buy one?' the American says.

'Sorry. All these are already promised to people.'

'Why didn't you catch any more?'

'With these, I have enough to support my family.'

'Did it take you long to catch them?'

'Not really, no.'

'What do you do with the rest of your time?'

'I play with my kids, take a siesta with my wife, hang out with my friends in the evening.'

'If you fished for longer, you could make more money. A lot more money. With that money you could buy a bigger boat, catch more fish, make more money, buy more boats, have a small fleet, make more money, buy a factory to process and distribute the fish, make more money, expand into other countries, float your company on the stock market and retire a multi-millionaire.'

'Retire? What would I do when I retire?'

'Whatever you liked. Play with your kids, take a siesta with your wife, hang out with your friends in the evening....'

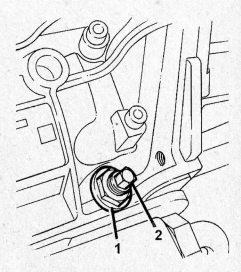

FIG 15•5 **SCREW LOOSE: WHAT YOU REALISE YOU MUST HAVE HAD ALL ALONG**

In the garage

Midlife crises often come hand-in-hand with marriage or relationship problems. Either can cause the other, and either can exacerbate the other. The breakdown of a relationship can help trigger a midlife crisis, or the crisis can put severe, possibly terminal, strains on that relationship.

If you've become a parent relatively late and therefore your children are still small, this can cause problems. Repeated singing of 'The Wheels On The Bus' would, after all, test the patience of a saint, let alone a frazzled middle-aged person who feels

that their best days are not so much behind them as a barely visible speck in the rearview mirror.

If your children are teenagers – well, we wrote an entire book about them, *Haynes Explains Teenagers*, and came to the conclusion that any sensible adult would just write off their children from the age of 13 onwards and check in again with them when they were 20. In the meantime, though, teenage children will be demanding money off you to go and have the fun you used to have, while carrying off the same kind of cool look you used to be able to, and

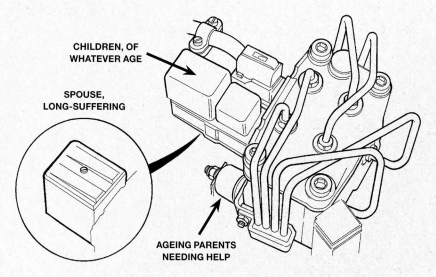

CHILDREN, OF WHATEVER AGE

SPOUSE, LONG-SUFFERING

AGEING PARENTS NEEDING HELP

FIG 15•6 **THE TIES THAT BIND: PLUGGING THE FAMILY UNIT**

while boasting metabolisms which seem annoyingly resistant to any calorie intake no matter how large, just like you used to.

Look on the bright side, though. If you think it's bad having to look at your children and see your past, it's much worse for them to be looking at you and seeing their future.

Is that helping? No? Thought not. Moving swiftly on, then.

Your children may have left home (this is not applicable if you're Italian, obviously, when sons in particular stay living with their parents until they're 35). For most of the past decade, this is the moment you've been waiting for: no more ghastly music, no more stroppy tantrums, no more monosyllabic grunts. But enough of what your wife thinks of you.

As it turns out, the only thing worse than having your kids around is not having them around. Now you and your spouse actually have to talk to each other, and sometimes you find you have less to say to each other than you thought (or at least less that is civil, interesting or both).

Again, the one-size-fits-all nature of the midlife crisis works here:

a) you've paid off most of your mortgage, so you have more disposable income and can dream of doing the things you've wanted to: or, alternatively, you're still mortgaged to the hilt, your house is falling down around your ears because you can't afford the necessary repairs, and you're seriously considering torching the place to claim the insurance.

b) your own parents, now presumably well into their seventies, are beginning to need you around more and more, and you feel responsible for caring for them, which in turn brings home to you that, just as you are now the age they were when you were a teenager, you will sooner than you think be the age they are now; or, alternatively, they're still disgustingly healthy, they're always off travelling or suchlike, and they seem to be having much more fun than you.

Research has shown that even chimpanzees and orang-utans – who don't in general have to worry about interest rates, rising damp or policing their offspring's Instagram account – suffer a downturn in mood and activity in the middle of their lifespan.

Spark plugs

No proper midlife crisis is complete without improper sex. If a midlife crisis is, among other things, about trying to recapture a lost youth, then reclaiming the sex life of that lost youth is high on the list of priorities – you know, the sex life you had before the demands of dealing with young children acted as a more effective desire suppressor than anything Big Pharma could have come up with, before getting drunk meant falling asleep on the sofa rather than partying all night, before a blue pill was a necessary precursor to horizontal action rather than one of two choices offered by Laurence Fishburne to

Keanu Reeves in *The Matrix*.

If you're going to go down the midlife sex route, you may as well fully embrace the cliché of it all.

> **'Some people ask the secret of our long marriage. We take time to go to a restaurant twice a week. A little candlelight, dinner, soft music and dancing. She goes Tuesdays, I go Fridays.'**
> *Henny Youngman*

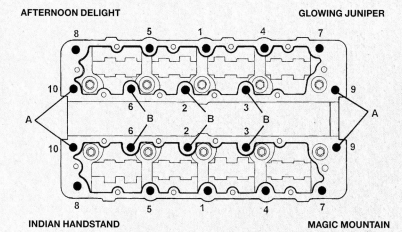

FIG 15•7 **SEXUAL POSITIONS INVENTED SINCE YOU LAST HAD CAUSE TO CHECK THE KAMA SUTRA**

⚠ For men

Your secretary

This ties in with the sense of dissatisfaction at work: who better to moan to than the person who knows the ins and outs (settle down at the back there, Beavis) of your working day? Behind the ruthless corporate shark beats the heart of a frustrated poet, or at least that's what you want her to think. In the office, you look smart and appear powerful. Wait till she sees you wrestling with an IKEA flatpack assembly at home and spending five hours putting together a table which would take a chimpanzee roughly five minutes.

Your au pair

Almost as big a cliché as the secretary. Where you can moan to your secretary that you feel unfulfilled at work, you can moan to your au pair that you feel unappreciated at home. Are they even called au pairs any more? Surely they've been jargonified, like everyone else, and are now Executive Childcare Managers, Domestic Arrangement Facilitators, or something similar? The phrase 'au pair' brings to mind a young French Isabelle Adjani lookalike, whereas nowadays they're more likely to be a frighteningly efficient Slovenian who doesn't just look after your children but has performed a time-

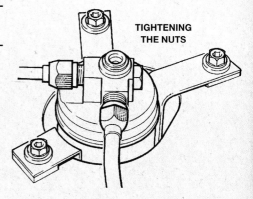

TIGHTENING
THE NUTS

FIG 15•8 **SEEKING CONNECTIONS**

and-motion study of all your household expenditure and put together a Powerpoint presentation which wouldn't shame a top management consultancy. Deep down, she's not after your body; she's after your job.

An old flame, who herself is going through a midlife crisis

This is the perfect synthesis of sex and nostalgia. You tell yourselves that you broke up first time round because you were too young, conveniently forgetting that time you shagged her sister and/or she shagged your best mate. You're both older and wiser now. Your respective sets of kids get on with each other, or at least they will do once they've got over the fact that the only thing worse than you having had sex with each other when you were the age they are now is you having sex with each other when you're the age you are now.

Women drivers

Though women are just as susceptible to midlife crises as men, they respond to them – if you'll forgive the massive generalisation, because it's the only kind of generalisation we do here at Haynes Explains – in rather different ways. Certainly in more dignified ways.

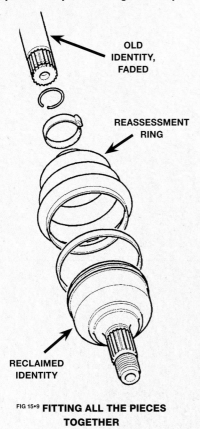

OLD IDENTITY, FADED

REASSESSMENT RING

RECLAIMED IDENTITY

FIG 15•9 **FITTING ALL THE PIECES TOGETHER**

Rather than trying to recapture their youth, they look upon midlife as a time for asserting an identity which might have been somewhat lost in the demands of careers and childrearing. The cynic would say that they're running towards something rather than away from it. Many women in midlife find that they no longer care so much about external approval or what other people think. In fact, you could argue that the female midlife crisis is not so much a crisis as a reappraisal.

A lot of male midlife crisis response is a solitary thing. Women, on the other hand, tend to be more collaborative than competitive. They realise that what you do is more important than what you own. They may put more effort into reviving friendships which work and motherhood have put on the back burner for a while. They might turn their energies to something creative – writing a novel, learning how to paint, trying pottery or sculpture. They might stand for parliament or do a masters degree. They might go travelling, the wilder and wackier the better – why lounge around on a beach in Greece when you could be driving a vintage car across Uzbekistan?

Of course, they might just shag their personal trainer instead.

⚠ **For women**

Your personal trainer

He's young. He's fit. He's got abs of steel and buttocks of granite and lots of other body parts of non-specific ferrous material. He gets to see you sweaty and flushed, so you're halfway to an affair already. Actually, he gets to manipulate your body too – 'no, you need to hold your leg like this' – so make that three-quarters of the way. Good news: you have a perfect excuse to see him several times a week. Bad news: so do the 32 other women also going through their own midlife crises. To be honest, it's amazing the man can still walk, let alone run around in a state of superfitness.

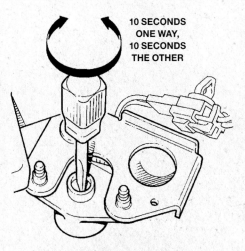

10 SECONDS
ONE WAY,
10 SECONDS
THE OTHER

FIG 15•10 **PERSONAL TRAINER STRETCHING KIT**

Your newly arrived work colleague, especially if more junior to you

No, you're very happy to show him the ropes, that's absolutely no problem. Yes, of course you're free to go out for a drink after work with him: it's important to get to know colleagues outside the work environment too. Yes, it would be wise to book a hotel room for the night of the upcoming train strike so you can be in work the next day. No, you had no idea that London has 100,000 hotel rooms and this is the only one left, so you'll have to bunk up with him.

An old flame, who himself is going through a midlife crisis

This is the perfect synthesis of sex and nostalgia. You tell yourselves that you broke up first time round because you were too young, conveniently forgetting that time you shagged his best mate and/or he shagged your sister. You're both older and wiser now. Your respective sets of kids get on with each other, or at least they will do once they've got over the fact that the only thing worse than you having had sex with each other when you were the age they are now is you having sex with each other when you're the age you are now.

Servicing required

This being the 21st century, sex is as much an online pursuit as anything else. For many midlife-crisis sufferers, internet dating is a brave and rather strange new world. When they got together with their spouses, courtship was a simpler thing: get hammered, wake up with each other, decide that you didn't find them totally repulsive, get married. Now it's all smartphones and the binary brutality of swipe left/ swipe right.

If you're dipping your toes into online dating for the first time in middle age, here are a dozen tips to help you get the best out of it.

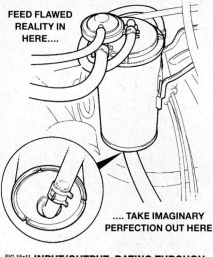

FEED FLAWED REALITY IN HERE....

.... TAKE IMAGINARY PERFECTION OUT HERE

FIG 15•11 **INPUT/OUTPUT: DATING THROUGH AN INTERNET SERVICE PROVIDER**

a) 'NSA' stands for 'no strings attached' not 'National Security Agency.' This is not a Jason Bourne movie, and you're not being tracked by operatives somewhere in a bunker.

....

b) Whether or not you smile in your profile picture is directly related to the state of your teeth. If you have Hollywood dentistry, knock yourself out. If your teeth look like badly maintained gravestones, maybe a sultry pout is better.

....

c) The only thing worse than putting up a picture of yourself with your ex is putting up the same picture badly cut off to exclude said ex (e.g. with a rogue arm around your shoulders, or the rip line from where you tore it still visible). In fact, make sure you're the only person in your pic, full stop. A group shot of you with your mates just ensures that your date will fancy one of them instead.

....

d) Your picture should have been taken within the last couple of years, so it's recognisably you. Some profile pictures are old enough to vote. You don't look like that any more. Depending on the skill of the original photographer, you may never have looked like that in the first place.

e) Don't be tempted to knock five years off your age or add three inches to your height. The truth will out sooner or later, and if any online date does lead to a new relationship, having to wear stack heels at all times and keep your driving licence and passport hidden will seriously cramp your style.

....

f) Think carefully when filling in the 'information about yourself' section. Every person out there loves travel, movies and hanging out with friends, so don't put that. On the other hand, your obsessive and frankly niche interest in Serial Killers of the Northwest USA 1965–82 is probably best left until a second date (which you will certainly not have if you bust it out first time round).

WARNING

Don't send naked pictures to someone unless (a) you've slept with them already (b) they've asked you too. For men, dick pics are 100% a no-no. If you really must send a dick pic, send a photo of Dick van Dyke/ Emery/ Nixon/ Francis/ Cheney instead. This way, the recipient will just think you're weird rather than gross.

'Looking for cuddles' does not mean 'looking for sex': it means 'looking for emotional affirmation'. 'What are you into?' does mean sex rather than books or TV programmes.

....

g) Don't take it personally when someone doesn't want a second date. It probably is their problem rather than yours. Online dating's a numbers game. You'll get more misses than hits.

....

h) Google yourself beforehand, because they sure as hell will. If you share your name with a disgraced local politician, be sure to make it clear that it's not you. If you share your name with an attractive singer – well, chances are you'll be rumbled the moment you walk in the door.

....

i) Always have a backup plan, especially on a first date. A coded text to a friend who can then ring up and pretend to be one of your children who needs you immediately gets you out of an awkward date without needing to be rude.

....

j) If someone texts you frantically Monday to Friday but never at weekends, they're married.

Boys and their toys

Four-year-old boys like playing with models of sports cars. 44-year-old men like playing with the sports cars themselves.

Sports cars are in almost every rational way a terrible choice of transportation for someone suffering a midlife crisis:

a) A man who has trouble getting up from a sofa is hardly going to fare better getting out of a low-slung driver's seat – and no, a commando roll onto the pavement as though this were the opening credits of *The Professionals* is going to fool no one.

b) Sports cars demand feline reflexes, which is fine when you're a Grand Prix driver with perfect eyesight but less so when you're a CFO who has to hold a menu at arm's length even to have a decent crack at deciphering it

c) A sports car won't make you any happier. It really won't. At best, it'll make you equally unhappy at a higher speed.

d) It is a penis extension, no matter how much you try to deny it. It is. It really is.

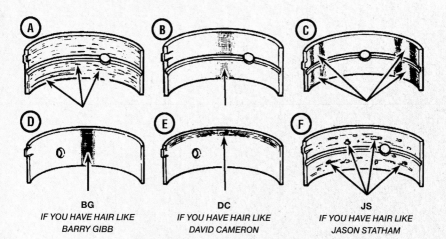

BG
IF YOU HAVE HAIR LIKE BARRY GIBB

DC
IF YOU HAVE HAIR LIKE DAVID CAMERON

JS
IF YOU HAVE HAIR LIKE JASON STATHAM

FIG 15•12 **OPTIMUM POSITION FOR WIND DEFLECTOR VIS-À-VIS HAIR LOSS**

e) Sports cars often, though not always, mean convertibles. Aside from the fact that a convertible is in essence a ludicrous proposition in a country that has the second worst weather in the world after Denmark, it is an even more ludicrous proposition when you consider the state of the average middle-aged man's hair. Nothing makes thinning hair look even more thinning than the equivalent of sticking your bonce in the path of a hurricane. It's the automotive equivalent of a comb-over. Yes, you can wear a baseball cap, but baseball caps on men of a certain age are also a poor idea. Exhibit A: *that* photo of William Hague.

f) Every boy racer from here to Timbuktu will try it on with you. You know the scene. You're sitting at the lights when up draws a Subaru with a rear spoiler the size of Heathrow, an exhaust pipe bigger than the Channel Tunnel and an engine which makes AC/DC at Knebworth sound like a library. Boy racer glances across and raises an eyebrow. You shouldn't bite. You know you shouldn't. But you're in a penis extension, and so he's challenging your manhood. When the lights turn green you both rocket off the line with Murray Walker's voice in your head shouting 'it's go!

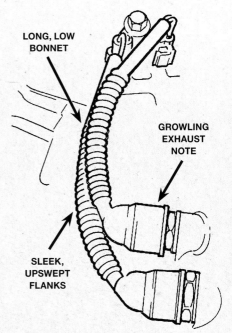

LONG, LOW BONNET

GROWLING EXHAUST NOTE

SLEEK, UPSWEPT FLANKS

FIG 15•13 **THE SPORTS CAR AND YOU: HOTWIRING YOUR SENSE OF MANHOOD**

Go! Go!' Half a mile down the road is a police car, and the next thing you know it's a year's driving ban, £1,000 fine, and self-same sports car sitting in your garage gathering dust next to a trickle charger while you wait out your suspension.

At least you can afford the insurance, though.

Two wheels, not four

You could go one step further and two wheels fewer, ditching the car for a motorbike. The wisdom of this decision depends very much on whether or not you were a biker beforehand. If you weren't, then this is dangerous territory. Not only do you have to pass a test, which means doing it at least 200 miles from home so no one you know is liable to see you wobbling around through the cones behind an instructor as though you were a six-year-old at their first ski lesson, but then you have to calculate

the trade-off between the kind of bike you want (either a supersports fire-breather or a muscular cruiser) and the kind of bike you have the experience and skill to handle (a Vespa). Either stands a good chance of killing you: the former in obvious ways, and the latter through a slower but relentless drip feed of shame. The only people who should ride Vespas are young Italian men with thin moustaches, fake gold earrings, gelled hair and an encyclopaedic knowledge of chat-up lines.

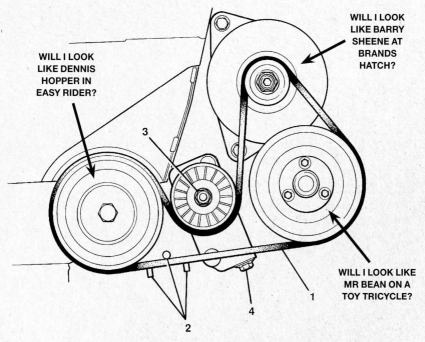

WILL I LOOK LIKE BARRY SHEENE AT BRANDS HATCH?

WILL I LOOK LIKE DENNIS HOPPER IN EASY RIDER?

WILL I LOOK LIKE MR BEAN ON A TOY TRICYCLE?

FIG 15•14 **THE GYROSCOPIC EFFECT: BUYING A MOTORBIKE IN MIDLIFE**

If you were a biker before...

...then midlife crisis biking is much more acceptable. In particular, you can meet up with other bikers on a Sunday morning, safe in the knowledge that at least 80% of them will also be suffering a midlife crisis, and zoom around country lanes for a couple of hours while imagining yourself as part of an earthbound version of the Ride of the Valkyries helicopter scene from *Apocalypse Now*. These kind of excursions are also prime opportunities to relive old stories from outings gone by, and bikers – like soldiers – are very good at spotting the Johnny-come-lately bluffer who talks the talk but manifestly didn't walk the walk. If you want to wax lyrical about the time you and your mates rode the Brecon Beacons, you'd better have actually done it, because someone will know that you should have taken the B4235 out of Chepstow rather than the B4293, and they will expose you for the Walter Mitty fantasist you so clearly are.

All midlife-crisis biking must, for maximum cliché value, be accompanied by the rider humming 'Born To Be Wild' to himself. The fact that 'Born To Be Mild' is substantially nearer the truth is neither here nor there.

Boats

Don't. Just don't. The second happiest day in a man's life is when he buys a boat, and the happiest is when he sells it. Besides, mate, the largest body of water within 75 miles of your house is the puddle which forms in that bit of the pavement where the council have forgotten to replace the paving stone for the 7,236th day running.

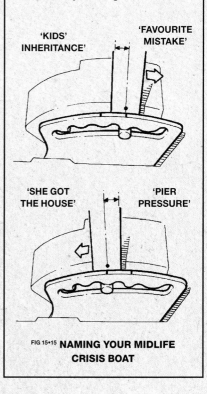

'KIDS' INHERITANCE'   'FAVOURITE MISTAKE'

'SHE GOT THE HOUSE'   'PIER PRESSURE'

FIG 15•15 **NAMING YOUR MIDLIFE CRISIS BOAT**

Performance

'It is a truth universally acknowledged,' as Jane Austen would have said had she been around today, 'that a man undergoing a midlife crisis will turn to exercise.' And not just any old exercise, either. Hardcore exercise, the kind that ticks every aspect of the midlife crisis psyche:

a) A ridiculously difficult challenge that if overcome brings out the inner Tarzan in any man, especially if he thought that Tarzan was long gone.

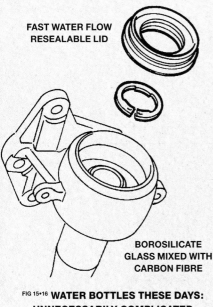

FAST WATER FLOW RESEALABLE LID

BOROSILICATE GLASS MIXED WITH CARBON FIBRE

FIG 15•16 **WATER BOTTLES THESE DAYS: UNNECESSARILY COMPLICATED**

b) The chance to buy absurdly hi-tech and expensive kit. In the olden days, men used to walk across continents clad either in thick woollen three-piece suits or a mix of aertex shirts, empire shorts and Dunlop Green Flash. Now you're legally forbidden from running any more than 5k without donning a vest which wicks sweat, keeps you cool in heat and warm in cold, makes the tea and would probably fly the space shuttle given half a chance.

c) Getting in shape = a boost to male vanity.

d) Planning. So much planning. Men love planning. All these kind of races come with equipment lists as long as your arm, route maps, terms and conditions, rules and regs, and so on. This is midlife male heaven.

e) The chance for some MASSIVE humblebragging on social media. 'Thanks to everyone who helped me raise lots of money for a very worthwhile cause by pushing my body to its limits and beyond. I will be functionally incontinent for the next fortnight, and the unblistered parts of my feet are in a serious minority, but I feel GREAT!'

⚠ Extreme driving

If hardcore exercise isn't enough, then there's always proper thrill-seeking for Midlife Crisis Man:

Run with the bulls in Pamplona

Actually this seems to be 98% drinking to 2% running, with the running unsurprisingly some distance off Olympic standards due to the vast amounts of premium Spanish lager consumed. Hard not to root for the bulls in situations like this.

Climb a very high mountain

Kilimanjaro's the obvious one, because it's basically a walk – a very long and high walk, granted – which you can then parlay into feats of derring-do when you return home. Probability of coming across an array of B-list celebs also climbing Kilimanjaro for a reality TV show and/or charity fundraiser: high. (Also, don't listen to Toto. They claim in their song 'Africa' that 'Kilimanjaro rises like Olympus above the Serengeti', even though they're 200 miles apart. If you're wandering round the Serengeti looking for a big mountain, don't blame Haynes, blame Toto.) If Kilimanjaro's too low and weedy for your tastes, then why not go for the Daddy of them all, Everest?

Swimming the Channel

This combines ultra endurance with the thrill-seeker's challenge of remaining alert enough to avoid a whole array of hazards en route, including but not limited to cross-channel ferries, supertankers, marine debris, seasickness, diesel fumes, jellyfish, hypothermia and David Walliams.

Heli-skiing

Go up over mountain in a helicopter. Affix skis. Jump out. Ski all the way down mountain. Probably best not to try this on Everest itself, though inevitably someone has (though he climbed up first – most helicopters can't fly that high – and skied all the way down to base camp without stopping). Yes, you guessed it, he was a middle-aged father of three (only 38 at the time, so clearly getting his midlife crisis in early).

Any of the frankly sectionable pursuits which take place under the aegis of being British and wacky. Exhibit A: the Bognor Birdman (attempt to fly off the end of Bognor Pier). Exhibit B: cheese rolling (follow an 18lb wheel of Double Gloucester down a steep hill, as fast as you can). Exhibit C: carrying flaming barrels of tar through the streets of Ottery St Mary in Devon. No, me neither.

High performance

The acme of midlife-crisis endurance sports is the Ironman Triathlon: a 2.4-mile swim, a 112-mile bike ride and a marathon.

First, the name: Ironman. Slightly undermined in recent years by Robert Downey Jr. in a red and yellow metallic superhero suit, but anyway. Ironman. There's not a chap alive who wouldn't jump at the chance of introducing himself with his name followed by the word 'Ironman'.

Second, the opportunity to secure not just one set of wildly expensive kit but three sets. A wetsuit for the swim. A wetsuit is just a wetsuit, right? Wrong! A wetsuit can be specially designed to scythe through the water with the ease and intent of a basking shark, which is nice but also slightly irrelevant when after a couple of miles in the water your swimming style is more Exhausted Lassie than Hungry Jaws. Then the bike leg, and here's where you can really go to town. Carbon-fibre bike frames alone can cost several grand, let alone wheels, pedals, handlebars, skinsuits and so on. All hail the guy who turns his nose up at all this and rocks up with a Raleigh Chopper, a pair of cut-off denim jeans and a Turkish Delight by way of in-ride sustenance.

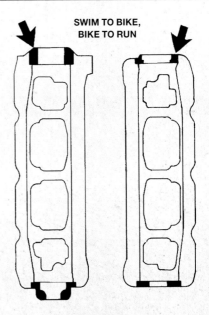

SWIM TO BIKE, BIKE TO RUN

FIG 15•17 **THE TRANSITION PEN: A SCHEMATIC**

Thirdly, the run. Super lightweight racing shoes with special bouncy soles and all that jazz. Yes, they'll make you run like Mo Farah, but only in the most basic sense that you're putting one foot in front of the other at more than walking pace.

Finally, an Ironman requires so much training – between 25 and 30 hours a week – that you won't have the time or energy to wonder why you're doing it in the first place.

⚠ Other midlife crisis sports

The Marathon des Sables

A week in the Sahara averaging out at a marathon a day, including a savage double marathon midway through, which is reputedly enlivened by the local kids nicking the luminescent route markers at night. Start out believing you're Lawrence of Arabia. End up believing you're Laurence Llewellyn Bowen. Keep yourself going for the last two days purely through the prospect of throttling the race director live on Eurosport.

L'Etape du Tour

Ride a Tour de France mountain stage the same as the professionals. Well, almost the same. The same stage, but (a) you don't have to do it day in day out for three weeks (b) you're not taking more drugs than Keith Richards. L'Etape has the highest concentration of MAMILs (Middle-Aged Man In Lycra) anywhere in the world.

Common or garden ultramarathon

These take place pretty much every weekend somewhere in the country, and vary in length and duration. There's a particularly tough one in Dorset which involves 82 (very hilly, coastal cliff) miles in 24 hours, and in a moment of delicious sadism ensures that the runners will pass through Weymouth town centre late on Saturday night, where their exhausted delirium will not be improved by the 'encouragement' of inebriated gentlemen participating in their own triathlon of furious drinking, kebab eating and freeform punch-ups.

Tough Mudders and similar

A mix of cross-country race and assault course. Typical ingredients: mud (obviously), hills, more mud, walls to climb over, cargo nets, barbed wire, electric shocks, and so on. A chance for adults to get as muddy on one day a year as their young sons get every day of the year.

WARNING

Extreme sports will in the long run make you look younger (though beware of 'gym face', when you look not so much chiselled as gaunt and unwell). In the immediate aftermath of any extreme sport, however, you will not look well. You will look bloody awful, like a cross between someone after a huge night out and a Marine in Vietnam who Has Seen Too Much.

Sound systems

If you can see a midlife crisis man coming (see 'Vehicle Appearance'), you can certainly hear him coming. Midlife radio stations are Radio 2 ('loving the show, Steve and gang') and Radio 4 ('and now over to Ambridge for *The Archers*'). Midlife-crisis radio stations, on the other hand, are 6 Music (all the trendy indie stuff) and Radio 1 (important to be down with the kids, even though nothing, literally nothing, embarrasses the kids as much as their parents liking the same music as them. This is, of course, an excellent reason to do it).

Midlife crisis music tastes can involve:

a) Getting really into bands whose members and entire fanbases weren't even born till you finished university.

....

b) Going to 80s or 90s nostalgia reunion tours of the bands you used to love then in a blatant attempt to recapture your youth. Yes, everyone says they're going 'ironically'. No, no one ever is. If you liked Spandau Ballet or Heaven 17 back in the day, just say so. You know all their lyrics, after all.

....

c) Wanging on about how the charts used to be an integral part of Sunday late afternoon/early evening, and how you got to be a dab hand at recording them while anticipating when the DJ would start talking over the end of the track and pressing 'pause' just beforehand. For bonus points, discuss the respective merits of (a) 90-minute cassettes vs. 120-minute (b) TDK vs. BASF.

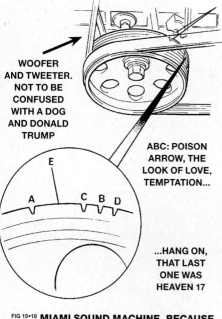

WOOFER AND TWEETER. NOT TO BE CONFUSED WITH A DOG AND DONALD TRUMP

ABC: POISON ARROW, THE LOOK OF LOVE, TEMPTATION...

...HANG ON, THAT LAST ONE WAS HEAVEN 17

FIG 15•18 **MIAMI SOUND MACHINE, BECAUSE SKEGNESS SOUND MACHINE DOESN'T HAVE QUITE THE SAME RING TO IT**

d) Lyrics. Very important to memorise them, especially for rap tracks, and then repeat them in time to the music with appropriate hand and head gestures (you know, that head-jerking-back-and-forth movement which you think makes you look like a man with funk in his soul but actually looks like a chicken wondering where their latest meal of layer pellets has gone).

e) Starting a band. You won't be short of bandmates, obviously, all of whom will suffer from the same perception-reality gap vis-à-vis their own talents as you do. Let's say you're the drummer. In your own head, you're Keith Moon. In fact, you're nearer Keith Harris' Orville. The band is liable to be so bad, your practice sessions so long and loud, and your Friday night residencies down the local pub so excruciating, that your wife will soon wish you were just having an affair instead. At least that way she'd get some nights to herself.

Then again, how much of a crisis can it be if you're forever three decades younger than Mick Jagger?

Festivals

Going to music festivals is the acme of any midlife crisis. A few years before, when your midlife had not yet reached crisis point, the very idea of Glastonbury or the like would have brought you out in hives, quite literally. The queues! The tents! The mud! The noise! The Portaloos! You would have emigrated to avoid these things. But now you're there like a pig in shit (also quite literally, probably) punching the air, filming with your phone, and posting Instagram pics captioned 'it's all getting a bit messy'. Be careful not to get all that, er, 'mud' on the cream seats of your sports car on the way home.

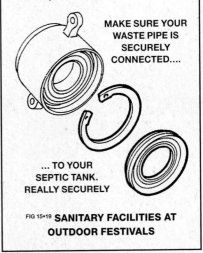

MAKE SURE YOUR WASTE PIPE IS SECURELY CONNECTED....

... TO YOUR SEPTIC TANK. REALLY SECURELY

FIG 15•19 **SANITARY FACILITIES AT OUTDOOR FESTIVALS**

Vehicle appearance

It can't be a proper midlife crisis without radically changing your dress code.

Before

You dress your age. Your shirts have collars, and you probably tuck them in (your shirts to your trousers, that is, not your collars to your shirts). You wear corduroys or jeans, generously cut for the fuller-figured man. Brogues or deck shoes. A blazer if you're feeling like being a touch smart, a leather jacket if not. Your look is basically one of two: country prep school headmaster or Jeremy Clarkson.

After

You dress half your age. T-shirts with the name of a band which is achingly trendy in a small part of downtown Seattle and totally unknown everywhere else. Jeans which hang halfway down your arse for that trademark Rikers look and you really have to work at this one, because your arse is not the arse you had 20 years ago. The arse you had then was as flat as a sheet of A4. The arse you have now is so large it could hold up a skyscraper without needing additional support. You wear trainers which cost as much as a Michelin-starred meal or snakeskin cowboy boots which make you look an unutterable berk.

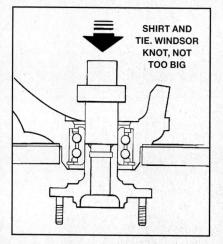

SHIRT AND TIE. WINDSOR KNOT, NOT TOO BIG

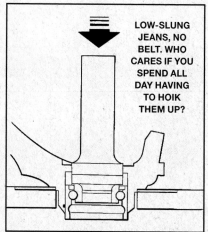

LOW-SLUNG JEANS, NO BELT. WHO CARES IF YOU SPEND ALL DAY HAVING TO HOIK THEM UP?

FIG 15•20 **DRESS SENSE, PRE- AND POST-CRISIS**

⚠ Tattoos and piercings

A couple of decades ago, these would have screamed midlife crisis like few other things. Nowadays, however, both body art and metallic adornments are much more common, and so the midlife crisis man can simply pretend to have had either or both all along. In turn, this means that tattoos are no longer the act of free-spirited rebellion they once were.

There are still some tattoos you should avoid:

a) Anything which hasn't been spellchecked;

b) Anything in a foreign language which hasn't been proved to be grammatically correct;

c) The name of your wife (she might not be around that long when she sees that the previously untouched white areas of your skin look like the graffiti-covered wall of a railway siding);

d) The name of your new girlfriend (she might not be around that long either when you come out the other side of this crisis);

e) The tattoo of a tribe to which you don't belong. Intricate Samoan or Maori tattoos look great – on Samoans or Maoris. They don't wear ones saying 'CFC 4 EVA', so don't wear theirs.

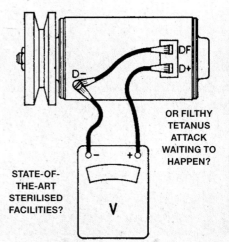

OR FILTHY TETANUS ATTACK WAITING TO HAPPEN?

STATE-OF-THE-ART STERILISED FACILITIES?

FIG 15•21 **MAKING SURE THE TATTOOIST KNOWS WHAT HE'S DOING**

Piercings

Similarly with piercings. An earring or nose stud is bog standard now. In the words of writer David Quantick (himself a middle-aged man, of course), 'even a safety pin through the cheek won't cut it. You have to look as though you've just had your entire head magnetised seconds before running through Rymans.'

Worn and bald tyres

Hair is a huge bone of contention for middle-aged men. It's not necessarily true that men lose hair as they grow older: more that they have the same amount of hair than ever, but that the hair tends to go looking for new places to be. For every strand which one day is no longer to be found on the scalp, there's one which has popped up on your eyebrows (now the density of the Amazonian rainforest), on the shoulders, the back, the chest, in the ears, up the nose, on your feet – why do you even need hair on your feet? – or a variety of other places over which we shall draw a veil as this is a family book and you're all adults.

There are several ways to deal with male pattern baldness. Only one of them actually works and that's embracing it. You're losing your hair? Big deal. Roll with it. Cut the rest of it short so it doesn't show too much. Or just shave it all off and go bald. It's worked for Bruce Willis and Jason Statham, hasn't it?

WARNING

Trying to look young is the fastest way to grow old. Don't try and look younger than you are. Try to look the best version of the age that you are.

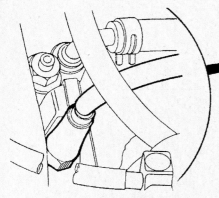

MIX LLAMA WOOL, FIBRE OPTIC LEDS AND AN OLD DRINKING STRAW

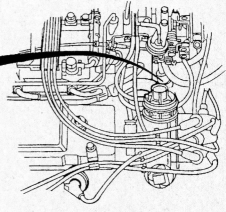

FIG 15•22 **BEHIND THE SCENES AT THE HAIRWEAVE FACTORY**

⚠ Advice and guidance

Don't wear a ponytail
It doesn't look cool. It doesn't make you look like a rock star (it does make you look like their roadie, though).
It looks as though, if someone grabs that ponytail and gives it a good yank, the whole lot will come off at once.

Don't have a comb-over
Think Bobby Charlton in his heyday. Fabulous footballer. Poor choice of coiffure.

Don't have a hair transplant
No matter how well it's done, the top of your head will still look like an arty drone photo of crops being planted in GPS-regulated squares.

Don't wear a wig
Just don't. Some of them look so like a doormat that they may as well have 'Welcome' written on them. The only wig you can wear is one of those ginger-hair-and-tartan-beret Scottish ones, and strictly for comedy value.

Don't go for the high and tight
Shaved at the sides, longer on top. There should be a law banning anyone over the age of 30 from having these. If a government can enforce legal purchase age for booze and tabs, it can enforce this. Sort it out.

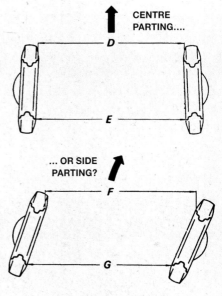

CENTRE PARTING....

... OR SIDE PARTING?

FIG 15•23 **HAIRSTYLING WITH LIMITED RESOURCES**

If you're going grey, embrace it. Seriously. Don't go all Grecian 2000 and dye it blacker than the dress code at a Sisters of Mercy concert. Pulling off the silver fox look is one of the few genuine pleasures left to a middle-aged man.

⚠ Fault diagnosis

Fault	Diagnosis	Treatment
You're not having a midlife crisis yet	You haven't reached the target age yet	Just wait. Just you wait
You can't read the menu. Or the newspaper	You have age-related hyperopia	Reading glasses, mate
You can't get out of a chair unaided	This is only the start of it	Install a winch next to your chair
You feel stuck in a rut	You probably are stuck in a rut. Marriage, job etc	Do things which energise you. No, not like that. At least not with someone who's not your spouse
You're not getting enough sleep	You have to get up three times every night to pee	Welcome to the rest of your life
You feel insecure in your job	Those bright young things you hired are now angling for your position	Sack them before it's too late. *Oh. It is too late*
Your children demand that you read the same things over and over to them	Your children are toddlers	They'll grow out of it
Your children regard you as a cashpoint with apparently fascist views	Your children are teenagers	They'll grow out of it
You are having improper thoughts about your secretary/au pair	You are a man having a midlife crisis	Walk away before it's too late. *Oh. It is too late*
You are having improper thoughts about your personal trailer/junior colleague	You are a woman having a midlife crisis	Walk away before it's too late. *Oh. It is too late*
You meet four different potential partners each week, all of whom are unsuitable	You are on an online dating site	Stop lying about your age, for a start
Someone is making a hand gesture which suggests that you are no stranger to self-abuse	You are driving in a sports car	What did you expect? You deserve this, to be honest
You are in a field surrounded by people half your age	You are at a music festival	Wave your hands in the air like you just don't care

Conclusion

The good news about a midlife crisis: it doesn't last. It really doesn't. Plenty of research has been done into happiness being shaped like a 'U' – it tails off in one's forties and then gradually begins to rise again. Carl Jung saw middle age as a time of rebirth rather than decline, a time when a person's masculine and feminine parts came together. (He may or may not have been a fun guy to be stuck with at a party.)

There are plenty of positive aspects to a midlife crisis too:

a) You may become more curious about yourself and the world around you, more open to new ideas and ways of doing things.

....

b) You may realise what (and who) you value in your life and what and who you don't, allowing you to discard behavioural patterns and friends you feel no longer bring you benefit.

....

c) You may realise that searching for happiness doesn't always, or even usually, lead you to it, but that happiness might come to you only once you stop looking; if you put your life in order, happiness will follow.

Ameliorate the effects

Meditate It can reduce anxiety, improve concentration and lead to better physical health.

Minimise your exposure to social media That picture you put up of you on a boat with your new girlfriend, crystal blue seas all around and a stunning sunset behind you – that doesn't show all the angst and heartache and confusion which has come along with your crisis. But when you see other people's pictures just like yours, you assume their lives are perfect in the ways yours isn't. Few things can make you feel inadequate like other people's social media feeds.

Online forums, on the other hand, can be helpful You'll soon find that whatever you're feeling is by no means new or unusual, and those who've been through it before are on hand to offer support and advice.

Be grateful for what you have rather than resentful at what you don't It's the biggest cliché in the world, but like all clichés it is so because it's true: other people are worse off than you are.

Titles in the Haynes Explains series

Now that Haynes has explained the Midlife Crisis, you can progress to our full size manuals on car maintenance (including a variety of sports cars), *Ferrari engines* (just need the car), *Shed Manual* (escape to your man cave or she-shed), *Slow Tech Manual* (slow down) and *Sleep* (time for a siesta).

There are Haynes manuals on just about everything – but let us know if we've missed one.

Haynes.com